DISASTERS

TITANIC

Kathleen Fahey

GARETH**STEVENS**
GS
PUBLISHING
A WRC Media Company

Please visit our web site at: **www.garethstevens.com**
For a free color catalog describing Gareth Stevens Publishing's list
of high-quality books and multimedia programs, call 1-800-542-2595 (USA)
or 1-800-387-3178 (Canada). Gareth Stevens Publishing's fax: (414) 332-3567.

Library of Congress Cataloging-in-Publication Data

Fahey, Kathleen, 1961-
    Titanic / Kathleen Fahey.
       p. cm. — (Disasters)
    Includes bibliographical references and index.
    ISBN 0-8368-4499-8 (lib. bdg.)
       1. Titanic (Steamship) 2. Shipwrecks—North Atlantic Ocean.
    I. Title. II. Disasters (Milwaukee, Wis.)
    G530.T6F34   2005
    910'9163'4—dc22   2004056710

This edition first published in 2005 by
Gareth Stevens Publishing
A WRC Media Company
330 West Olive Street, Suite 100
Milwaukee, Wisconsin 53212 USA

Original copyright © 2004 The Brown Reference Group plc. This U.S. edition
copyright © 2005 by Gareth Stevens, Inc.

Project Editor: Tim Cooke
Consultant: Don Franceschetti, Distinguished Service Professor, Departments
of Physics and Chemistry, The University of Memphis, Tennessee
Designer: Lynne Ross
Picture Researcher: Becky Cox

Gareth Stevens series editor: Jenette Donovan Guntly
Gareth Stevens art direction: Tammy West

Picture credits: Front Cover: Library of Congress.
Corbis: Bettmann 9, Eric and David Hosking 19, Matthew McVay 25, The Mariners
Museum 14, Ralph White 4, 8, 27; Getty Images: 5, 21, 26; Library of Congress: title
page, 7, 11, 13, 15, 16, 17, 18, 22, 23, 24; National Archives: 12; Photos12.com: 20th
Century Fox/ Paramount 29; Rex Features: 28; Topham: Picturepoint 10, Public
Record Office/HP 20.

Maps and Artwork: Brown Reference Group plc

Printed in the United States of America

1 2 3 4 5 6 7 8 9 09 08 07 06 05

ABOUT THE AUTHOR

American-born Kathleen Fahey has been writing children's books on a
wide range of subjects for over fifteen years. She now lives in England
with her young family, which "test-drive" all of her books.

CONTENTS

1 TRAGEDY IN THE ATLANTIC

The *Titanic* set sail on its maiden, or first, voyage from Great Britain to New York, with a stop in Ireland, in April 1912. After just three days at sea, it hit an iceberg and sank. More than 1,500 of the 2,224 people on board died.

The people who built the *Titanic* said that it was unsinkable. It was designed to be the safest ship of its time. It was also famous for its great luxury. On the upper decks, there were huge staircases and grand dining rooms for first-class passengers. Many famous people were on board, including John Jacob Astor, from one of America's richest families. There also were many other millionaires on board.

▼ The *Titanic* sets sail on its maiden voyage to New York. It left Southampton, in southern England, shortly after midday on April 10, 1912.

4

There were **aristocrats** as well, including Lady Duff-Gordon. Also on board was Bruce Ismay, whose family ran the White Star Line, which owned the *Titanic*.

▼ A London newsboy carries an announcement of the *Titanic* disaster.

Other passengers traveled in second or third class. Third class, or steerage, was not very comfortable. The cabins were six decks down, deep inside the ship. The steerage passengers were not allowed to be in first-class areas. **Immigration** laws in the United States said that the

TITANIC DISASTER 'GREAT LOSS OF LIFE EVENING NEWS

Patterson Elementary
3731 Lawrence Dr.
Naperville, IL. 60564

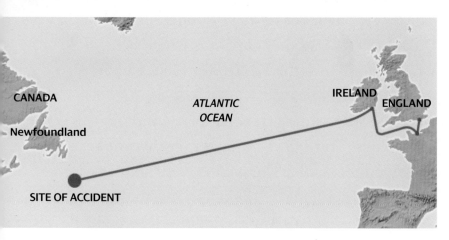

◄ **The planned route of the *Titanic* took it southwest across the Atlantic. The ship struck the iceberg and sank about 400 miles (644 kilometers) off the coast of Canada.**

groups must be kept apart, in case steerage passengers had diseases.

The passengers came from 25 countries. There were about 300 Americans, 300 British people, and many people from Sweden and Ireland. Many had left poor countries such as Bulgaria to make a new life in America. Most of the immigrants were in steerage class.

After the ship took on more passengers in Ireland, Captain Edward J. Smith set sail into the Atlantic on April 11, 1912. The seas were calm, but the temperature fell as the ship got nearer to Newfoundland, in Canada. There was a church service on Sunday, April 14. On most ships, lifeboat drills were held on Sundays, but Captain Smith did not hold one.

THE ICEBERG

During the day, the *Titanic* received warnings from other ships about icebergs. That evening, however, only two officers were put on watch.

FACT FILE

WHERE:

Atlantic Ocean, 400 miles (644 km) south of Newfoundland, Canada

WHEN:

About 11.40 P.M. on April 14, 1912

TOTAL TIME:

About three hours

INTENSITY:

Loss of ship

COSTS:

$7 million (cost of ship in 1912 dollars) plus cargo and personal possessions

KILLED OR INJURED:

More than 1,500 killed

They had lost the **binoculars** that helped them see over great distances.

At about 11:40 P.M., one of the men saw a huge iceberg about one mile (1.6 km) ahead. He signaled the **bridge**, where officers tried to turn the ship. They threw the engines into reverse to slow it down, but the *Titanic* was steaming ahead at about 25 miles (40 km) per

EYEWITNESS

"Suddenly a queer quivering ran under me, apparently the whole length of the ship. Startled by the very strangeness of the shivering motion, I sprang to the floor. With too perfect a trust in that mighty vessel, I again lay down. Some one knocked at my door and the voice of a friend said, "Come quickly to my cabin. An iceberg has just passed our window. I know we have just struck one."

– Elizabeth Shutes

THE CAPTAIN'S STORY

After the disaster, many people blamed Captain Edward J. Smith for causing the accident. They said he was traveling too fast in an area where there were icebergs. Many people on the ship, however, thought Smith was a hero. He helped passengers to escape and did not try to save himself. He followed the old tradition that a captain went down with his ship. Captain Smith was last seen on the ship's bridge as water rose above his waist.

▲ **Captain Smith posed for this picture the day before the *Titanic* set sail from Southampton, England.**

▶ The lifeboats were stored on the upper deck of the *Titanic*, near the ship's funnels, which are smokestacks.

hour, too quick to stop before the ship hit the iceberg. The ship was able to turn some and scraped past the iceberg on its right side. Most people did not realize what had happened.

The *Titanic* stopped while the **chief engineer** inspected the damage. He told the captain that the ship would sink in about an hour and a half. Just after midnight, the captain ordered the lifeboats to be prepared.

INTO THE LIFEBOATS

By about 12:15 A.M. on April 15, passengers were pouring onto the deck. Some were still in their pajamas. The ship was leaning toward the

THE SHIP'S BAND

One of the most famous stories about the sinking of the *Titanic* is about the musicians on the ship. They usually played to entertain the first-class passengers. While the lifeboats were being loaded, the band played on deck. They played favorite tunes and jolly ragtime music to keep people calm. Later, they played hymns. The musicians kept playing as long as they could. They went down with the ship.

left. Officers ordered women and children to get into the lifeboats first, but some men got into the boats as well. No one really knew what was going on. Some people stayed on deck. They still thought that the *Titanic* could not sink. Some lifeboats were only half full when they were lowered into the water. As the ship leaned over more and more, people began to fight to get into the lifeboats that were left.

After the captain's order to prepare the lifeboats, steerage passengers deep inside the ship tried to find a way up to the deck where the boats were kept. Many people lost their

▶ This picture was painted soon after the disaster. It shows the deck of the *Titanic* as people prepared to get into the lifeboats. In reality, the scene was full of panic and confusion.

way or were trapped by doors that were locked to keep them out of first-class areas.

The lifeboats, full of women and children, were lowered into the freezing cold waters of the Atlantic Ocean. Some men jumped into the boats as they were being lowered. Other men said goodbye to their wives and children. The officers began firing signal rockets into the sky in the hope that another ship might spot them.

The *Titanic* had been sending emergency messages by **telegraph**. No ships were close by. Finally, a message came from the *Carpathia*, a British liner only 58 miles (94 km) away. It

▼ **These sketches of the *Titanic* sinking were made by a survivor who watched the event from a lifeboat.**

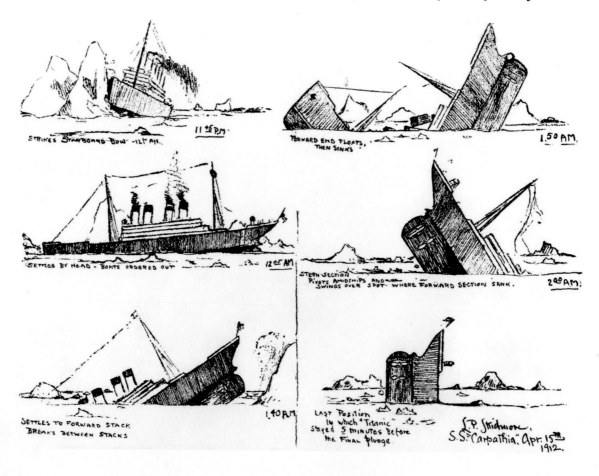

► An artist's recreation shows how the lifeboats got as far away from the ship as possible to avoid being sucked under as the *Titanic* sank.

had missed earlier distress calls but was now making for the *Titanic* as hard as it could.

On the *Titanic*, people panicked as the last lifeboats were lowered. One officer fired a gun into the air to stop a crowd from rushing one of the boats. Captain Smith told his crew, "Now it is every man for himself."

THE END OF THE SHIP

In the lifeboats, people were frightened and confused. Many boats did not have a ship's officer on board, and many boats had no lights, but the lights of the *Titanic* still lit up the sea. Most people realized that they needed to row away quickly. When the *Titanic* sank, the force would suck down anything nearby.

EYEWITNESS

"Our lifeboat, with thirty-six in it, began lowering to the sea. This was done amid the greatest confusion. Rough seamen all giving different orders. As only one side of the ropes worked, the lifeboat at one time was in such a position that it seemed we must capsize in midair. At last the ropes worked together and we drew nearer and nearer the black, oily water."

– Elizabeth Shutes

The *Titanic*'s bow (front) was under water. Many survivors said that the *Titanic* tipped almost straight up in the air before it sank. Others said that it broke in half.

There were still more than a thousand people on board. They jumped into the icy sea. Some were sucked down with the ship, while others held on to floating **debris**. Some people tried to swim to the lifeboats, but the boats were too far away.

The people in the lifeboats could hear cries for help from the people in the water. The horrible sound haunted them for the rest of their lives. The water was so cold that a human could only live about 20 minutes before

► Survivors from the *Titanic* talk on board the *Carpathia*, which picked them up on the morning of April 15, 1912.

dying of **hypothermia**. Some people in the boats wanted to row back to pick up survivors, but others did not. They thought that the boats would sink if they had too many people in them. Slowly, the cries for help faded as people in the water died. The lifeboats floated quietly in the dark and waited for rescue.

The *Carpathia* arrived at 3:30 A.M. The captain had prepared the ship's dining rooms as hospital areas. At 4:00 A.M., he saw a green signal rocket from one of *Titanic*'s lifeboats, about one-fourth of a mile (0.4 km) away. The *Carpathia* rescued all the passengers. As dawn broke, the other boats were scattered over a wide area. As they rowed to the *Carpathia*, some survivors cheered, but others were silent from shock and grief. Many survivors were so weak or cold they had to be lifted up onto the ship. By about 9:00 A.M., all 705 survivors were on board. The *Carpathia* headed for New York.

◄ This *Titanic* lifeboat was photographed by a sailor from the deck of the *Carpathia* just before the survivors were picked up.

2 THE CAUSES OF THE DISASTER

There were several reasons why the *Titanic* sank and why so many people died. Passengers had been told that the great ship was unsinkable. That claim proved to be false.

The *Titanic* was built using the best **technology** of the time. The ship had an outer covering, called a hull, that was made from sheets of steel that were about 1 inch (25 millimeters) thick. The ship also had a double-layered bottom. The hull was divided into sixteen watertight compartments. The bulkheads, which are walls separating the compartments, had huge doors that could be closed if the ship's hull filled with water. The ship could still float even if four compartments were flooded, but **engineers** believed that the ship would never flood that badly.

▼ **This diagram of the *Titanic* shows the different decks and compartments deep inside the ship's steel body.**

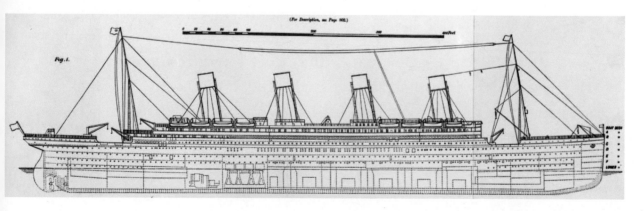

▶ **Steel walkways and platforms surround the *Titanic* as the ship is being built. Engineers felt that the ship's design would make it unsinkable.**

The engineers were wrong, however. When Thomas Andrews, the *Titanic*'s chief engineer, rushed to inspect the damage after the accident, he found that the ship had scraped past the iceberg for about 300 feet (90 meters). The iceberg had torn the steel plates off the ship's hull. The six front compartments were already filling with water. Because the walls between the compartments did not reach all the way to the ceiling, as one compartment filled, water spilled into the next one. That dragged the front of the ship down. As the front sank, water then spilled into the next compartment until the ship was flooded. The engineer saw at once the ship was sure to sink.

One of the reasons the ship suffered so badly in the accident may have been because

THE MISSING LIFEBOATS

▼ **The great promenade, or walking, deck was designed so that people could take long walks. Putting more lifeboats on the *Titanic* would have taken up much of that walking space.**

One of the worst parts of the *Titanic* disaster was that the ship did not have enough lifeboats. There were only twenty lifeboats for the 2,200 people on board. In part, this was because the ship's engineers and owners believed that the ship would never sink. Another reason for the shortage of lifeboats was that they took up too much room. The White Star Line was competing with other ship companies. They needed any advantage that would get passengers to travel on the *Titanic*. One feature was space on all of the decks for passengers to relax. Lifeboats took up too much precious deck space. According to the safety laws of the time, the number of lifeboats was set by the weight of the ship, and not by the number of passengers it could carry. That changed after the *Titanic* disaster. From then on, a lifeboat space was required for every person on board a ship.

of money. The *Titanic*'s owners, the White Star Line, had to compete against other ship companies. White Star tried to cut costs so that it could sell tickets as cheaply as possible, and the team that built the ship had to keep costs down. Although the bottom of the ship was made of two layers of steel, the hull was

only made of one. Engineers knew that a double hull had saved another ship, the *Great Eastern*, from sinking when it hit a rock in 1862, but the double hull was too expensive. Also, the bulkheads were not built to reach the ceiling, which left them open to flooding. In addition, the steel used to make the bolts that held the plates of the hull in place may not have been made from strong enough metal.

▲ The company that owned the *Titanic*, the White Star Line, owned several ships, including this ship docked in New York City. To be able to compete with other companies, the White Star Line had to keep their shipbuilding costs down.

INQUIRIES INTO THE DISASTER

There were two **inquiries** into the *Titanic* disaster, one in the United States and one in Britain. Both inquiries found that the direct cause of the accident was that the ship was moving too fast. If the *Titanic* had been going slower, there would have been time to avoid the iceberg.

The belief that the *Titanic* was unsinkable led the crew to take risks. The captain ignored warnings of ice. In the early evening, officers noticed it felt colder than usual, which was a sign that there might be icebergs nearby. The ship received another warning at 9:30 P.M. It said there were many icebergs directly ahead. When someone on another ship sent a warning about ice, the telegraph officer on the *Titanic* told him to "shut up." The *Titanic* steamed ahead at nearly full speed. Some people think the captain might have been ordered by the White Star Line to sail as quickly as possible.

► **The team of people in charge of the U.S. inquiry into the *Titanic* disaster question survivors in New York City.**

THE FORMATION OF ICEBERGS

Icebergs are huge blocks of ice floating in the ocean. They form when they break off from large sheets of ice in the Arctic Circle and Antarctica. Arctic icebergs, like the one that sank the *Titanic*, are smaller than Antarctic icebergs. Arctic icebergs can be as small as the size of a table or as big as a ten-story building. They break off from sheets of ice called glaciers that are slowly sliding across Greenland. Each year, Greenland produces about 10,000 to 15,000 icebergs. Most icebergs form during the warmer weather of spring and summer and stay in the far northern oceans, where there are very few ships. An average of 375 icebergs a year drift south of Newfoundland. There, they become a danger to shipping routes that cross the Atlantic Ocean.

▼ **Only a small part of an iceberg can be seen. A much larger part of it is under water.**

LOSS OF LIFE

Even though the *Titanic* could not avoid hitting the iceberg, more people could have been saved. Many died because no one knew what to do. There were not enough lifeboats for the passengers and crew, but many more people could have fit into the boats *Titanic* did have.

There had been no lifeboat drill. Many people did not know the way to the deck

► This emergency telegram was received on the Russian ship *Birma* just before the *Titanic* sank. The *Birma* was too far away to help. The *Californian* was the nearest ship to the *Titanic*, but its telegraph operator was asleep.

where the lifeboats were stored. It was difficult for the steerage passengers to get there. They could only reach the upper decks by long routes along many hallways and up staircases. The officer who helped steerage passengers escape gathered them into groups, but only one group reached the lifeboats. Others were stopped by locked doors or by guards who blocked their way. Only one-fourth of steerage passengers made it to the lifeboats. In contrast, nearly three-fourths of first-class passengers made it.

COULD ANYONE HAVE HELPED?

Both of the inquiries into the disaster asked whether other ships could have helped the

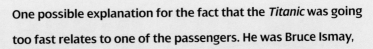

THE OWNER'S STORY

▼ **Bruce Ismay, chairman of the White Star Line, survived the disaster.**

One possible explanation for the fact that the *Titanic* was going too fast relates to one of the passengers. He was Bruce Ismay, whose family ran the White Star Line. Some people think that Ismay might have pushed the captain to go as quickly as possible. It would have looked good for the White Star Line if the ship's maiden voyage was as short as possible. Ismay had lunch with Captain Smith on the day of the disaster. He took great interest in the voyage. Ismay even showed other passengers a telegraph message he had been given warning the ship that there was ice ahead.

Titanic more. They concluded that one ship—the *Californian*—had been close enough to the *Titanic* at the time of the accident to have saved most, if not all, of the people on board. The *Titanic* had modern telegraph equipment. At about 12:15 A.M., it began sending a distress code, which at the time was the letters CQD.

Before the *Titanic* disaster, there was no rule that said someone had to watch a ship's telegraph machine at all times. On the *Californian,* the telegraph operator had just ended his shift and gone to bed. There was no one left to hear the *Titanic*'s signal. The inquiry team also said that the officers on board the *Californian* should not have ignored the signal rockets fired from the *Titanic*.

3 THE AFTERMATH OF THE DISASTER

The sinking of the great ship *Titanic* on its first voyage shocked the world. Rules were changed to improve safety at sea. The story of the ship still fascinates people today.

The *Titanic* disaster was shocking partly because the ship had been thought to be unsinkable. Dramatic stories from survivors were printed in every newspaper. Many people told stories of the brave passengers and crew who went down with the ship. People were also shocked that a number of famous people had died. Many people looked down on Bruce Ismay, of the White Star Line, for saving himself rather than giving up his place in the lifeboat.

SAFETY AT SEA

As a direct result of the *Titanic* disaster, a meeting called the First International Convention for the Safety of Life at Sea took place in London in 1913. At the meeting, rules were made about

▼ The *New York World* newspaper announces the disaster on the morning of April 16, 1912.

22

TITANIC LIFE BOATS ON WAY TO CARPATHIA

▲ In 1912, a newspaper put together this collection of pictures as a souvenir for its readers. It shows a telegraph operator, lifeboats at sea, the *Titanic*, and a lifeboat drill. In the center is a picture of Captain Edward J. Smith.

traveling safely by sea. The rules dealt with many of the things that had gone wrong during the disaster. The laws declared that all ships must have a lifeboat space for every person carried on board. There also had to be regular lifeboat drills during every voyage, so that all of the passengers and crew would know where the lifeboats were and how to get there.

Another new rule was that all ships had to have a telegraph operator on duty at all times. In 1914, World War I began, so the rules were not put into effect yet. They were put into effect after the war ended in 1918.

FAMOUS SURVIVOR

▼ Margaret Brown was one of the most famous survivors of the *Titanic* disaster.

Among the survivors of the disaster was an American woman, Margaret Tobin Brown. She had run for Congress, even though women in the United States were not yet allowed to vote. She also studied languages. After the ship sank, Brown used her ability to speak several languages to help survivors from other countries. She also became the head of a group formed to help other survivors. Later, she became an actress. In 1960, a musical play was written named *The Unsinkable Molly Brown*. The main character was based on Margaret Brown. In 1964, the play was made into a movie of the same name.

A GRIPPING STORY

The story of the *Titanic* disaster has fascinated people ever since it happened. It still attracts more interest than perhaps any other disaster in the twentieth century. Many books have been written about it. There have also been several films made about the disaster.

Many plans have been made to recover what is left of the *Titanic*. People have hoped to raise the *Titanic* since it sank, but until recently, technology had not been good enough to do it. The ship rests on the seabed at a depth of about 2 miles (3 km). At such a depth, the **water pressure** is so great that special equipment is needed to dive to the ship. It is unlikely that the main parts of the ship could be raised today. They would probably crumble after sitting so long under the sea. Many people also believe that it would be wrong even to try to raise the *Titanic*, since

INTERNATIONAL ICE PATROL

▼ Members of the International Ice Patrol prepare a radio transmitter. They will drop the machine onto an iceberg to track the iceberg's path.

As a result of the *Titanic* disaster, the International Ice Patrol was set up in 1914. It is run from Argentia, in Newfoundland, Canada, by the U.S. Coast Guard. During the iceberg season, the patrol's two airplanes fly on long trips that last up to eight hours each. The pilots and **oceanographers** aboard the airplanes look out for icebergs near the Grand Banks, an area near Newfoundland. They spot icebergs and track their paths. If an iceberg is getting close to shipping routes, the patrol sends out a ship. It takes up position near the iceberg to warn other ships.

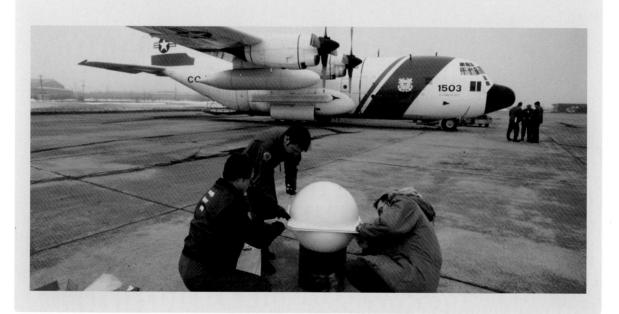

BREAKING UP ICEBERGS

For a long time, scientists have tried to find a way of breaking up icebergs that threaten ships. They believe that if they can break a large iceberg into smaller pieces, those smaller pieces will melt more quickly. In 1929, scientists did manage to blow up an iceberg by putting bombs on it. However, all later tries have not worked. Dropping bombs on icebergs or firing underwater missiles at them have not broken off enough ice to make any real difference. The International Ice Patrol has also tried covering part of an iceberg with black charcoal. The color black soaks up heat more quickly than the color white. Scientists thought that a black iceberg might heat up and melt. The black charcoal did not seem to make much difference, however.

▼ **Many icebergs are so big that it is difficult to break them up even when bombs are placed on them. Scientists are trying to come up with other ways to make them break apart.**

▲ In 1985, Robert Ballard's team photographed the front of the *Titanic* on the seabed nearly 2 miles (3 km) beneath the surface of the Atlantic Ocean.

so many passengers died on it. They say that the wreck is a tomb and so it should be left alone out of respect for the dead.

ROBERT BALLARD

After the wreck of the *Titanic* was found in 1985, a number of groups have explored what is left of the ship and brought many objects to the surface. Robert Ballard, who is a U.S. oceanographer, was the person who pushed hardest to find the ship. In 1985, he set up a trip with the French Oceanographic Institute, helped by the U.S. Navy. Ballard and his team found the *Titanic* using a remote-controlled **submarine**. The wreck was located 14 miles

(23 km) northeast of the place that had been given in the *Titanic*'s last distress message.

THE *TITANIC* ON THE SEABED

The first part of the ship Ballard saw was one of the **boilers**, which had broken free as the ship sank. The boiler lay in a field of debris from the ship about 600 yards (550 m) long. Nearby lay stained glass panels from the first-class smoking room, pots and pans from the kitchens, and lumps of coal from the boiler rooms.

In a trip the next year, Ballard used a submarine to photograph the wreck. He used other underwater ships to go inside the wreck and take pictures and videotape it. One important fact Ballard discovered was that the *Titanic* broke into two pieces as it sank, just as some witnesses had said. The bow (front) of the wreck is nearly in one piece but the stern (back) is almost destroyed. Ballard also found out that the iceberg had not cut a huge gash in the side of the ship, which is what everyone had thought. Instead, it ripped off the steel plates of the hull and broke apart the seams where the plates were joined together.

▲ **One piece of wreckage recovered from the** *Titanic* **is the binnacle, which is the housing for the ship's compass.**

RAISING THE *TITANIC*

Since Ballard's second trip to the *Titanic* site, other groups have also explored the wreck. They have recovered thousands of items from the seabed, including silverware, jewelry, eyeglasses, parts from the engines, and dollar bills. Many of the objects are on display in major museums around the world.

An exploration team in 1996 planned to raise part of the hull to the surface. Rough seas made the hull break off from the chains that were pulling it up. It sank back to the seabed. The *Titanic* is falling apart more and more, which makes future efforts to raise the ship from the seabed very unlikely.

In 1997, a new movie about the disaster was a great hit around the world. The movie's success proves that, even now, people are still touched by the sad story of the *Titanic*.

▼ The 1997 movie *Titanic* starred Leonardo DiCaprio and Kate Winslet. The movie used special effects to recreate the disaster, and also used recent footage of the wreck of the real *Titanic* on the seabed.

GLOSSARY

aristocrats People who belong to the upper classes of society and are often noble or very wealthy.

binoculars A handheld instrument with lenses that help make distant objects appear closer.

boilers Parts of a ship's engine in which water is heated to make steam, which drives the engines.

bridge The front section of a ship from which the captain and other officers steer the ship.

chief engineer The officer on a ship who is in charge of making sure that the ship's engines and other equipment work well.

compass An instrument that has a needle that always points to Earth's magnetic North and so is used to show direction.

debris Pieces left when something has been broken up or destroyed.

engineers People who are trained to work with engines or to make or build things.

hypothermia Very low body temperature; hypothermia can kill people in only a short time.

immigration The movement of people to live in a new country.

inquiries Official studies held by experts to discover facts about issues such as disasters.

oceanographer A scientist who studies oceans.

submarine A ship that is designed to travel under water.

technology The most up-to-date knowledge and machines that are available at a particular time.

telegraph A machine for sending messages by wires or radio over long distances.

transmitter a machine that sends out radio waves.

water pressure Force of water pressing on an underwater object from all sides; water pressure is greater at greater ocean depths.

FURTHER RESEARCH

BOOKS

Adams, Simon. *Titanic* (Eyewitness Books). Dorling Kindersley, 2004.

Alcraft, Rob. *World's Worst . . . Shipping Disasters* (World's Worst). Heinemann Library, 2000.

Kupperberg, Paul. *The Tragedy of the Titanic* (When Disaster Strikes). Rosen Central, 2002.

Landau, Elaine. *Heroine of the Titanic: The Real Unsinkable Molly Brown*. Clarion Books, 2001.

Major, Mireille. *Titanic: Ghosts of the Abyss*. Hyperion, 2003.

Matsen, Bradford. *The Incredible Quest to Find the Titanic* (Incredible Deep-Sea Adventures). Enslow Publishers, 2003.

Stewart, David. *You Wouldn't Want to Sail on the Titanic* (You Wouldn't Want to . . .). Franklin Watts, 2001.

WEB SITES

Encyclopedia Britannica Online Exhibit
search.eb.com/titanic/01_01.html

Encyclopedia Titanica
www.encyclopedia-titanica.org

National Geographic Kids: Titanic
www.nationalgeographic.com/ngkids/9607/titanic.html

RMS Titanic, BBC Southampton
www.bbc.co.uk/southampton/features/titanic/index.shtml

RMS Titanic, Inc.
www.titanic-online.com

Titanic Historical Society, Inc.
www.titanic1.org/

INDEX